The purpose of this study guide is to provide supplemental educational material. It is not intended as a substitute or replacement of THE POET X.

Published by SuperSummary, www.supersummary.com

ISBN – 9781072775218

For more information or to learn about our complete library of study guides, please visit http://www.supersummary.com

Please submit any comments, corrections, or questions to:
http://www.supersummary.com/support/

TABLE OF CONTENTS

PLOT OVERVIEW

Elizabeth Acevedo's award-winning 2018 young adult novel, *The Poet X*, brings to life the inner world of protagonist Xiomara Batista. Xiomara is 15 years old, and from her bedroom in Harlem, she writes poetry in order to put on the page all the feelings and ideas she cannot seem to be able to say out loud. Xiomara resigns herself to writing in her notebook and sharing her thoughts with only a few trusted individuals until her English teacher, Ms. Galiano, invites Xiomara to speak her words in a spoken word poetry club, and, later, at a citywide poetry slam competition.

Though this novel-in-verse takes place over only a few months during Xiomara's sophomore year in high school, Xiomara goes through many significant experiences, all of which are documented in her poetry. Xiomara begins to doubt the religious teachings of her childhood as she matures into a curious and bright young woman. She struggles with her developing body and its effect on other people, experiencing at the same time what it feels like to fall in love. As Xiomara experiments with independence, she observes that her need to separate from her parents is particularly challenging for her mother. Mami lives and breathes by her Catholic faith, and she has high expectations for Xiomara, expectations that are vastly different from the ones that Xiomara has for herself.

Against the urban backdrop of present-day Harlem, Xiomara, her twin brother, Xavier, and their friend, Caridad, grow up among drug-dealers and teenagers having babies well before they are ready to be parents. Their church is both a sanctuary and a jail for Xiomara, and she questions the teachings of the church with her characteristic incisive thoughtfulness. At school and on the street,

Xiomara is both a quiet presence and a highly conspicuous one; her womanly figure means she is noticed, but Xiomara wants to be known for her creative abilities—for her dreams and her intellect, not for her curves. Xiomara's relationship with her older parents is difficult, as they don't seem to understand her, nor do they trust her judgment. Her mother's devotion to the Catholic church means that Xiomara has to live up to Mami's religious ideals, and just as Mami is setting impossible limits on Xiomara's social freedoms, Xiomara falls deeply in love. She feels she must keep her romance with her biology lab partner, Aman, a secret, until everything becomes evident during the novel's intensely dramatic and emotional moment of climax.

Written in a musical and compelling combination of slang, colloquialisms, and formal poetic language, *The Poet X* is an unusual and sensitive book that honors the rhythms of hip-hop while taking the reader along on the rollercoaster ride that is adolescence. Through Xiomara's eyes, being a teenager has never been more challenging, but thanks to her insistence that she be true to herself, readers of all ages will learn that there is potential for beauty in every conflict. Love can take any number of forms, Xiomara learns, and the readers of her deeply-personal poetry are reminded of this inevitable fact of life with every stanza.

CHAPTER SUMMARIES AND ANALYSES

Part 1

Part 1: "In the Beginning Was the Word"

Part 1, Chapter 1 Summary: "Friday, August 24-Sunday, September 16"

In the first poem of the novel, Xiomara describes her neighborhood in Harlem as she reflects on the end of the summer. From her seat on her stoop, she sees "the old church ladies, chancletas flapping" (3), and listens to "honking cabs with bachata blaring / from their open windows" (3) as a group of drug dealers watch "girls in summer dresses and short shorts" (4). She goes inside when she knows it's nearly time for her mother to be home from work. Xiomara reflects on her appearance, her mother's warnings about boys, and her name, which means "[o]ne who is ready for war" (7). According to Xiomara, her mother found her birth difficult, unlike the birth of her twin brother, Xavier, so an unusual name that "labors out of some people's mouths" (7) feels appropriate to her.

Xiomara's mother works as a cleaner in Queens, and she passes the time on her commute by "reading verses / getting ready for the evening Mass" (11). Mami, a devout Catholic, wants Xiomara to be confirmed, but Xiomara doesn't know how to tell her that Jesus now feels like a friend "who invites himself over too often, who texts me too much" (13). Her doubts about the church are founded in a sense that Catholicism "treats a girl like me differently" (14); Xiomara writes, "all I'm worth is under my skirt / and not between my ears" (14). When Xiomara tells Mami she wants to wait to be confirmed, Mami threatens to send her to the Dominican Republic, "where the priests and nuns know / how to elicit true piety" (17).

Xiomara reflects on being born to older parents who had given up on the idea of having children: "You will be hailed a miracle" (18), they tell Xiomara, which will become emotionally burdensome to her. Her father, Papi, stops drinking, but that doesn't make Mami forgive him for "making her cheat on Jesus" (23) by marrying her.

In confirmation class with her friend, Caridad, who has just returned from the Dominican Republic, Xiomara sits with a look on her face that "announces I'd rather be anywhere but here" (24). Father Sean, who teaches the class, "tells us we're going to deepen / our relationship with God" (25); instead of listening to Father Sean, she whispers to Caridad, distracting her with questions about boys and kissing. Caridad is Xiomara's oldest friend, and though she is "all [Xiomara's] parents want in a daughter" (30), Caridad "isn't all extra goody-goody in her judgment" (31). Instead, Caridad supports Xiomara with all of her questions, telling her that "she knows / I'll figure it all out" (31). Xiomara worries about her new interest in boys and their interest in her, and she wonders what will happen if she "like[s] a boy too much and become[s] addicted to sex" (32). She also worries about becoming "angry and bitter like Mami" (32) and wants to know how to "figure out the weight / of what it means to love a boy" (33).

On the first day of school, Xiomara walks to Chisholm High School, where she "greet[s] security guards by name" (35) as she enters the building that offers her "a way to get closer / to escape" (36). She meets her English teacher, Ms. Galiano, who makes a positive impression on Xiomara. As Xiomara prepares to write about "the most impactful day" (38) of her life for an English assignment, she remembers the day she got her first period, when she was 11 years old. That day, Mami "backhanded me so quick she cut open my lip" (40) because Xiomara had tried to use tampons and "'[g]ood girls don't wear'" tampons (40). She turns in an essay that describes the leather notebook her brother, Xavier, gave her for their birthday, in which she writes every day, "dress[ing] my thoughts in the clothing of a poem" (41).

After school, Xiomara goes home to do the chores Mami has assigned her. Xiomara's twin, Xavier, who goes to a special school for gifted students, "helps [Xiomara] when he's home" (42), though he is not expected to and "he won't get in trouble if he doesn't" (42). Xiomara reflects on Xavier's easy way with Catholicism, which she links to the fact that he was named for a saint. She writes about how her mother compares her to her twin, especially when she gets into a fight; Xiomara doesn't explain to Mami that she fights on behalf of the gentle and quiet Xavier, against "other kids / [who] tried to make him into a wound" (45).

Less than a week after the start of the school year, Xiomara finds herself frustrated. At this stage, tenth grade is much the same as ninth grade, and she still feels "like a lone shrimp / in a stream where too many are searching / for someone with a soft shell / to peel apart and crush" (46). Boys pay Xiomara attention for her womanly body, her mouth, and her eyelashes "that are too long / so they make me almost pretty" (48). She imagines herself as the daughter of Medusa, whose "looks stop men / in their tracks" (48). Later, Xiomara, Caridad, and Xavier watch a basketball game, and Xiomara notices that Xavier is "staring as hard as I am at one of the ballers" (50). When one of the boys speaks to her, Xiomara feels self-conscious: "although I like to look, I hate to be seen" (50). When the player insults her, however, Xiomara retorts with a sharp comment, and "the dudes around us start hooting and hollering in laughter" (51).

At this moment, Xiomara reflects on the attention she receives from men and boys, who feel "they can grab themselves / or rub against me / or make all kinds of offers" (52). These intrusive encounters happen all the time, enraging Xiomara, and she calms herself by listening to music and writing "all the things I wish I could have said" (53). In this particular case, however, Xiomara feels most disappointed in her twin, who stands by during these confrontations and "never defends" her (54).

The following Sunday, Xiomara unwillingly goes to church with her family. When the time comes to take communion, Xiomara "feels bolted to the pew" (56) and her mother pressures her to go "take God" (56) and "thank him for the fact that you're breathing" (56). She refuses, thinking of her doubts in God and Jesus and men in general, who are "the first ones to make me feel so small" (59).

At home, Mami is angry and punishes Xiomara by insisting she attend evening Mass with Mami every night that week. When Xiomara overhears Mami and Papi discussing her behavior, she hears Papi explain to Mami that "[t]eenage girls are overexcited. / Puberty changes their minds" (63). Xiomara knows that Papi's insight into the ways of young women comes from the days before she and Xavier were born, when Papi "tossed his seeds to the wind, / not caring where they landed" (64). Though Papi has stopped chasing women, choosing to work hard and provide for his family instead, Xiomara feels that his presence "doesn't mean he isn't absent" (65).

Part 1, Chapter 2 Summary: "Monday, September 17-Friday, September 21"

Xiomara spies an announcement for a spoken-word poetry club that "feels personal, / like an engraved invitation / mailed directly to me" (67). Though the club meets on Tuesdays, at the same time as her confirmation class, Xiomara doesn't give up hope. In biology class, she finds that she is drawn to her lab partner, Aman, especially when "his forearm touches" Xiomara's (69). Later, Xiomara tells Caridad about Aman, describing him as cute and telling her that his arm is warm. Caridad is scandalized, believing that Xiomara's mention of Aman's warm arm is "code for something" (72). At home, Xavier has found the poster about the poetry club that Xiomara has saved. He places the poster carefully on her bed, saying to his sister that "'[t]his world's been waiting / for your genius for a long time'" (73). Unfortunately, Xiomara knows that her time on Tuesdays, "for the foreseeable future, / belong to church" (73).

At school the next day, Xiomara asks Ms. Galiano about the spoken-word poetry club. Her teacher explains that spoken word is poetry that is memorized and performed. When Xiomara watches the video of a performance that Ms. Galiano shows the class, "[t]he poet talks about being black, about being a woman, / about how beauty standards make it seem she isn't pretty," and Xiomara "feel[s] like she's talking directly to me" (76). Ms. Galiano encourages Xiomara's interest in the club, but Xiomara is incredulous at the thought of competing at a poetry slam; after all, Xiomara "only speaks to get someone off [her] back" (79). In the bathroom, after her shower at home that night, Xiomara recites one of her poems out loud, just to feel what it's like. When Mami asks her about what she is doing, she says she is "memorizing verses" (79).

In biology class, Xiomara and Aman talk about "measurements and beakers" (81), and, eventually, music. Aman mentions he likes hip-hop artist Kendrick Lamar and suggests they "listen to his new album together sometime" (81). Xiomara reflects on the power of music later, marveling at how "music can become a bridge / between you and a total stranger" (83). That night, Xiomara dreams of Aman. In the dream, "his hands move so close, our faces move closer" (85), and the next day, Xiomara can't "look Aman in the face" (87). When her nerves settle, she suggests to him that they listen to the Kendrick Lamar album the next day. Xiomara frets about Mami's dating rules as she anticipates her "non-date" (88) with Aman, knowing that "going to a park / alone with Aman / might as well be / the eighth deadly sin" (91). The morning of her non-date with Aman, Xiomara holds her happy secret close, feeling powerful in her body as she irons her shirt, "[a] for-sure sign I'm scheming / since I hate to iron" (92).

Part 1, Chapters 1-2 Analysis

The first part of the novel introduces the main characters and their relationships with one another. Xiomara, the protagonist, discusses the meaning of her name by way of a self-introduction. Because she is a quiet person, it might seem ironic that her name means "one who is ready for war"; her personality within the context of her environment, however, is actually combative and warrior-like as she finds herself defending her weaker twin brother and standing up for herself on a regular basis. As a young girl, growing up on the streets of Harlem, she toughened up quickly, but as she moves through adolescence, living under the constraints of conservative and religious parents means that her combative side has a different kind of battlefield to navigate. Xiomara's tough exterior masks a remarkable sensitivity and softness; she cares deeply for her family, and she thinks deeply about her choices, so she's easily hurt by her mother's many injustices and easily perturbed by the illogical course her life can take at various turns.

According to Xiomara's characterization of her family, her mother's strictness and her dogmatic stubbornness makes living with her parents difficult for Xiomara. She also struggles with her father's disengagement, which is poorly timed; the one man from whom she needs attention is ignoring her, while strange men all around her give her far too much attention. Xiomara's intense desire to know what it's like to have a boyfriend is ironic; her curiosity about the opposite sex is set against a backdrop of inappropriate and unwelcome sexual attention that she receives from men and boys no matter what she wears or how she walks. Xiomara resents this attention because it feels disrespectful and belittling. Feeling small under the male gaze is difficult because the experience devalues her other qualities, like her intelligence and her generous spirit. When she meets Aman in biology class, however, Xiomara falls in love quickly, indicating an unexpected emotional openness in this young woman who perceives herself as unknowable.

Xiomara is so busy trying to survive adolescence herself, complete with confirmation classes, that she does not notice her twin brother's difficulties. In an ironic twist of fate and characterization, Xavier is the more devout twin, but he is just as interested in boys as his sister, an interest that both Mami and the Catholic church will surely find sinful. Caridad, the twins' friend and confidante, represents the tolerant side of religion, as she has a non-judgmental and loving relationship with both Xiomara and Xavier.

Ms. Galiano is a role model for Xiomara; she is a smart and confident Latina who loves poetry as much as Xiomara does. She is small in stature, but strong, and in this way, she might remind Xiomara of Mami. Unlike Mami, however, Ms. Galiano nurtures Xiomara's sensitive and inquisitive personality with her many invitations to Xiomara to share her thoughts and feelings in her English assignments.

Part 2

Part 2: "And the World Was Made Flesh"

Part 2, Chapter 1 Summary: "Sunday, September 23 - Friday, October 19"

At the park, Xiomara and Aman "sit on a bench with more / than our forearms 'accidentally' rubbing" (95) and listen to music for an hour. Afterwards, they walk to the train holding hands, and Xiomara is "truly thankful / that this city has so many people to hide" her (96).

In several poems about Xavier, Xiomara describes him as "the only boy I will ever love" (97) because he is "the best boy I know" (97). He is also "the worst Dominican" (98) because he doesn't worry about looking cool or any of the other concerns that weigh on a stereotypical teenage boy. Xavier goes to a school for gifted students, so "his book smarts meant / I couldn't even copy his homework" (99). Though the twins are close, "[h]e doesn't get sympathy pains" (100), but "every now and then, he'll say, in barely a mumble, / something that shocks the shit out of" Xiomara (101). Xavier notices that Xiomara "look[s] different" (101) after her afternoon with Aman, but then he explains that the change must be due to her menstrual cycle.

Aman and Xiomara swap phone numbers and text each other while they are apart. They pass each other flirtatious notes during biology class. At home, Xiomara writes poems about Aman while her family carry on as normal, though she does notice that Xavier appears "happier than he usually looks" (103). At school, Xiomara suspects that Ms. Galiano knows she has "been secretly practicing" (104) spoken word at home. Xiomara writes in her journal at lunchtime, sitting with her group from the year before at "a table full of girls that want to be left alone / ...Sharing space, but not words" (104). In confirmation class, Xiomara thinks about Aman and whispers to Caridad. One day, while waiting for Xiomara, Mami notices she is distracted during class. Mami lectures Xiomara on the importance of paying attention to "la palabra de dios" (108) while "sweat breaks out on [Xiomara's] forehead" (108). Ms. Galiano writes Xiomara a note praising her poetic style and inviting her again to the poetry club. The note pleases Xiomara but reminds her of the fact that the meeting time on Tuesdays conflicts with her confirmation class.

On Friday afternoon, while Xiomara and Aman are at the park, he asks her to read him one of her poems. She's nervous, but after telling him he "better not laugh" (111), she reads him a poem about Papi. Aman compliments her writing, telling her that her poem "[m]akes [him] think of [his] mother being gone" (112), a confession that takes their relationship to a new level. Aman explains that when he and his father moved to New York City, his mother stayed behind in Trinidad, promising to join him and his father eventually, but she never came; now, she only "calls every year on [Aman's] birthday" (114). When it's time to go, Xiomara and Aman walk together silently, hand in hand, "[e]ach of us keeping / the other warm against the quiet chill" (116).

A few weeks pass and the weather cools. Ms. Galiano continues to invite Xiomara to the poetry club. Aman and

Xiomara walk to the train after school each day; Xiomara privately questions how Aman feels about her because "he never presses too hard" (117). At church, Xiomara takes the communion wafer and hides it "beneath the pew" (118) because she feels too much distance from God to take communion. On Tuesdays, Xiomara struggles while sitting in confirmation class instead of in poetry club. Usually, she sits quietly, but one day, she decides to ask Father Sean about Eve and her "parable [that] teach[es] us how to deal with temptation" (119). Xiomara challenges Father Sean in front of the entire class, and when his "face has turned as hard as the marble altar" (121), he suggests they speak after class. Caridad warns Xiomara not to say too much in case Father Sean speaks to Mami, so when Father Sean tries to encourage Xiomara to speak openly about her questions, Xiomara "tell[s] Father Sean I won't ask about Eve again" (125).

Xiomara drafts out ideas for her essay for Ms. Galiano, wishing she could write about herself as "the warrior she wanted to be" (126) but turning in an essay about her imagined future accomplishments instead. In her essay, Xiomara describes a center for young women that she has opened and the house in the Dominican Republic she has bought for her parents.

In biology class, Xiomara and Aman hold hands inside their desk, "[h]is hand lighting a match / inside my body" (129). Xiomara writes a poem about "a heat I have no name for" (130) that she experiences at night, and the release she feels that brings her "shame / [that] settle[s] like a blanket / covering me head to toe" (130).

Part 2, Chapter 2 Summary: "Tuesday, October 16-Friday, November 9"

Aman asks Xiomara about church one day while they are walking to the train calling her by his nickname for her: "X" (132). She explains that her mother "is big into church / and I go with her and to confirmation classes" (133), but she is "into poetry" (133). When Aman asks her what her stage name is, she replies "maybe I'd be the Poet X" (133) and his expression of approval, "said by the right person / by a boy who raises [her] temperature" (134) makes her "[s]woon" (134).

Though Xavier knows Xiomara is "texting so late into the night that the glow / of my phone is the only light / in the whole apartment" (135), he doesn't ask about it until Xiomara asks him if the reason he is smiling more has "a name" (137). The twins make a plan for Halloween; Xiomara later texts Caridad to invite her along.

The next time they meet after school, Aman asks Xiomara if she has "ever smoked a blunt" (140). She says no, and Aman "settles his hand on [her] thigh" (140).

The following Tuesday, "[t]he day that becomes THE DAY/ starts real regular" (142). Xiomara and Aman cut classes when a fire alarm rings with only 30 minutes left of school. At the park, they share Xiomara's first kiss; she writes later that "my heart is one of Darwin's finches learning to fly" (145). At her train stop, Aman asks her if she wants to go out this weekend, to Reuben's Halloween party, but she doesn't answer, distracted by "too many things to say and nothing to say at all" (147).

Xiomara goes to confirmation class feeling sure that "[a]nyone who looks at me / will know I know what it means to want" (149). She thinks of all the things she wants to do but can't, remembering that "Mami told me I'd have to pray extra / so my body didn't get me in trouble" (151). When she was younger, Xiomara hid her body "in big sweaters… / trying to turn this body into an invisible equation" (151) but now, she wants Aman "to leave his fingerprints all over me. To show all his work" (151). Noticing Xiomara's distracted state of mind, Father Sean talks with Xiomara about self-doubt, admitting his own experience with self-doubt to reassure Xiomara and to encourage her to speak openly about what she is thinking.

At home, Xiomara and Xavier talk while Xavier texts rapidly on his phone. When Xiomara asks him about his texting, he says, "'we both know we're messing around / and that Mami and Papi will kill us if they find out'" (155). Xiomara writes about the fact that their parents' expectations are different for each of them when it comes to dating and that they probably wouldn't mind if Xavier had a girlfriend; however, "I don't know what they would do / if the person he brought home was not a girl" (155).

Xavier comes home from school with a black eye, and Mami assumes that Xiomara is responsible for his injury. Xiomara is "heated / with Twin / for not telling me / someone at school / was bothering him" (160). She texts with Caridad, asking her if she can skip the weekend movie plan they made for Halloween so she can go to the party instead. Caridad agrees to help Xiomara, but warns her not to "get pregnant" (162). The night of the party, Xiomara leaves with Xavier, but then leaves him to take the train to Washington Heights, where Reuben lives. She waits for Aman and "ignore[s] the stares of a group of boys by the speakers" (164). When Aman arrives, they dance "exactly the way people do / in music videos" (166). Xiomara gets nervous and needs to take a break from dancing, so they go outside; Aman says that he lives nearby and that his father is at work. Xiomara feels shaky, and she gets up to go, but Aman "pulls [her] back down beside him" (168), asking her to read him a poem. On her way home, Xiomara texts Caridad to let her know she is on her way, telling Caridad that she has "a lot of feelings. But it was fine" (170).

On Monday after school, Xiomara takes a train downtown to Xavier's school to find out more about her brother's black eye. She sees Xavier with "a tall, red-haired boy, with fingers the color of milk" (173) who acts tenderly towards her brother. Xavier spots his twin sister and demands to know why she is at his school, telling her "'I don't need you to fight for me anymore'" (174). As they take the train home together, Xiomara wants to discuss "White Boy" (176), but Xavier only wants to play chess on his phone.

In a draft for an assignment for English class about a person misunderstood by society, Xiomara writes about Mami, who was her "hero" until Xiomara hit puberty and Mami's behavior towards Xiomara changed. She turns in an essay about Nicki Minaj instead, reluctant to confess her true feelings to her teacher. In English class, a member of the poetry club named Chris performs a short piece and tells the class about the citywide slam in February. Xiomara feels herself react: "I should be there. / I should compete" (183).

Aman and Xiomara go ice-skating on a day when school is off and Mami is at work, triggering in Xiomara the memory of an old birthday tradition: when they were younger, Mami would take the twins ice-skating for their birthday every year. Xiomara learns that Aman loves winter sports, so much so that he "made Pops pay / for a special TV channel so [he] could keep up" (186). When he was a little boy in Trinidad, he watched the Winter Olympics, and he tells Xiomara that he is "nice with the skates" (186). Xiomara invites Xavier to come with them, but he is still mad at her, so she goes to meet Aman alone. Aman amazes Xiomara with his confidence and his "turns and figure eights" (188), and Xiomara marvels at "all the things we could be / if we were never told our bodies were not built for them" (188).

On the train heading home after skating, Aman kisses Xiomara, and they embrace even though it's "too easy to run into someone from the block" and "people are probably staring" (189). As she walks home from the train station, Xiomara thinks about the addictive quality of her time with Aman, comparing herself to a junkie with "eyes wide with hunger" (191). When she arrives home, Xiomara hears Mami yelling and realizes that Mami witnessed her "make-out session on the train" (192) so she goes straight to her bedroom. Xavier comes in and finds her, but Xiomara is in such trouble that she "can't even be grateful / he's speaking to [her] again" (193).

While Mami and Papi yell at each other about Xiomara's behavior, she tries to "unhear / my mother turn my kissing ugly, / my father call me the names / all the kids have called me / since I grew breasts" (194). Xavier tries to help, but Xiomara refuses it, saying "I didn't do anything wrong" (197) as they hear the footsteps of their parents stop outside their bedroom door. When the confrontation between Xiomara and her parents begins, Mami drags Xiomara to her altar of the Virgin and demands that Xiomara pray to the Virgin Mary for forgiveness while kneeling on uncooked grains of rice. Xiomara compares herself to an ant that "will / survive / the / apocalypse" (201). As Mami yells at her and calls her a *cuero*, "[t]he Dominican word for *ho*" (205), Xiomara silently accepts her accusation, thinking to herself, "I am a cuero, and they're right. / I hope they're right. I am. I am. I AM" (205). Mami continues to yell, describing all men as dirty and reminding Xiomara that "Eve was easily tempted" (208). Mami hits Xiomara in the face over and over, making her feel dizzy and sick, and then "prays and prays" (209) while Xiomara writes poetry in her head "[t]hat has nothing to do with repentance" (210).

Afterwards, Xavier tries to comfort Xiomara with "a bag / of frozen mixed vegetables" on her knees and her cheek, telling her "don't get in trouble / until we can leave. / Soon we can leave for college" (213). Xavier tells Caridad what's happened, and they both show concern for Xiomara, but she wants to do nothing but "curl into a ball and weep" (215). Mami punishes Xiomara by taking away all of her freedoms, including her phone, but she doesn't know what she would say to Aman even if she could text him or call him.

The next day at school, Xiomara stands next to her locker in a fog, still overwhelmed by the events of the previous day. She doesn't notice a group of boys behind her until "one bumps me / both his hands palming and squeezing my ass" (218) in front of other students, including Aman. Xiomara pauses as "[e]verything inside [her] feels beaten" (218) and she hopes for a moment that Aman will stand up for her. To her disappointment, frustration, and, eventually, anger, Xiomara realizes that Aman is "not going to do a damn thing" (219). She shoves the guy whose hands were on her body and threatens him. As she walks away, she says to Aman, "'That goes for you too. Thanks for nothing'" (220).

Part 2 Analysis

Part 2 of the novel is full of important events in the plot line: Xiomara has her first kiss, she deceives Mami in order to meet Aman at the party, and she outwardly challenges Father Sean in confirmation class, finally giving voice to the rebellious thoughts in her head. Soon afterwards, Xiomara learns that Xavier has a boyfriend and that he has outgrown the need for her to defend him against bullies. Then, after Xiomara's recklessly passionate embrace on the train, Mami and Papi find out about Aman and the consequences are dire; Mami loses control of her emotions, damaging her relationship with Xiomara, perhaps irrevocably.

The emotional pace of the novel gathers momentum in this section of the book as the characterization of Xiomara as a poet builds. She begins to explore self-expression, using her voice to share her ideas and feelings just as she is experimenting with performing her poetry out loud. Though these verbal expressions can and do cause tension in some of her most important relationships, Xiomara cannot contain herself any longer; as she develops as an artist of spoken word, her words spill out necessarily.

Xiomara's decision to challenge Father Sean's rendition of the Adam and Eve story as a parable about the dangers of temptation signifies her sense of self as a young woman. She knows it's unfair for Eve to be blamed by the men of the Bible and she takes Eve's story to heart because it reminds her so much of her own story. As Xiomara questions the traditional gender roles of her parents and her church, she is not a hardened feminist: she wants the most important young men in her life—her brother, Xavier, and her boyfriend, Aman—to defend her in her most vulnerable moments. This desire does not reflect girlish weakness, however; rather, it reflects Xiomara's impatience with the unfairness of having to cope with situations where she must stand up for herself, over and over.

After Xiomara sees Xavier with Cody, she refers to Cody as "White Boy," revealing her own reluctance to accept someone who is different from her. Eventually, Xiomara refers to Cody by his name, giving him the respect he deserves as much as she does, which demonstrates growth in her character. That Xiomara can be so frustrated with injustice yet display racist tendencies herself ensures that she is a round character, complete with flaws and unattractive characteristics as well as the potential for change.

Part 3

Part 3: "The Voice of One Crying in the Wilderness"

Part 3, Chapter 1 Summary: "Sunday, November 11-Monday, December 17"

For the next few days, Xiomara shuts out everyone in her world, including Caridad, Xavier, and Aman. At church on Sunday, Xiomara asks Father Sean if she can give a confession under pressure from her parents. Xiomara "just want[s] to tell them, / it's NOT THAT DEEP" (225), so when she meets Father Sean and tells him what happened on the train, she admits to him that she's "'not sorry I kissed a boy. / I'm only sorry I was caught. / Or that I had to hide it at all'" (226). Father Sean understands that there is more to discuss, so he approaches Mami and suggests to her that Xiomara "keep / coming to classes[…] / but not take the leap of confirmation this year" (228). When Mami reacts badly to this idea, Father Sean reminds her that "'anger is as much as a sin / as any Xiomara may have committed'" (229). While talking alone with Xiomara, Mami is furious, comparing Xiomara to her father, "'a man addicted to women'" (231). Xiomara reflects in writing on her mother's anger and her feelings of heartache, but though she "spend[s] every class writing in [her] journal" (237), Ms. Galiano is concerned enough to send Xiomara to the guidance counselor. Xiomara overhears Mami making plans to take her to the Dominican Republic, which Xiomara views as "the ultimate consequence" (237).

In poem after poem, Xiomara works through her pain. She tries to think of Aman as nothing but "a failed rebellion" (238), but she knows in her heart that he was "everything" (238). When Xavier asks her to write a poem about love, Xiomara reacts angrily, assuming he wants the poem for his boyfriend, Cody, but Xavier only wants Xiomara "to write something beautiful for [her]self" (240). Caridad calls on the apartment landline, upset with Xiomara for ignoring her for two weeks, and tells Xiomara she's worried about her. On Thanksgiving Day, Mami finally returns Xiomara's cell phone, but Xiomara says she has "no one to text" (243).

After Thanksgiving, Xiomara drafts her ideas for an English assignment about "the last time [she] felt free" (244) as several poems. She remembers a time when she and Xavier were little and played "ninjas in volcanoes" (244), and a more recent moment with Aman, when she felt she "could / say something, anything, in this moment / and someone was going to listen" (246). She thinks of sitting on her apartment stoop, feeling the "freedom in choosing to sit and be still / when everything is always telling you to move, move fast" (247). In the end, Xiomara decides to turn in a paragraph in which she states that "[f]reedom seems like such a big word" (248). Ms. Galiano follows up with Xiomara to express her concern, mentioning poetry club again to Xiomara. This time, Xiomara decides to skip confirmation class to attend.

In biology class, Aman sits on the other side of the room; Xiomara's new lab partner is a girl named Marcy. Xiomara is "still angry that he didn't stand up for me / [but] a part of me feels like maybe I messed up, too" (254). They don't speak at all. When she goes to poetry club for the first time, she meets Isabelle, who "says whatever is on her mind" (256); Chris, who is "loud, a mile-a-minute talker" (257); and Stephan, whose writing style is "a fired visual, landing on target" (257). When Xiomara reads her poem out loud to the club members, she feels she is finally heard and that her words are important. Ms. Galiano also compliments her bravery and "for the first time since the 'incident' / [Xiomara] feel[s] something close to happiness" (260).

Xiomara and Caridad decide to go to a poetry open mic with Xavier, and they decide that Caridad will be the one to talk to Mami about it. At home, Xiomara notices that "Twin seems sadder / and sadder every day" (264). At school, Xiomara starts spending her lunch hour in the bathroom, writing poetry away from the prying eyes of other students, until Isabelle invites her to write with her at lunchtime in the photography room.

One afternoon, Xiomara goes home from school to find Xavier in tears, and, forgetting to call Mami to tell her she's home from school, she asks Xavier if it was Cody who hit him previously and gave him the black eye. Xavier explains that the black eye was from an accident in gym class, and his problem is so much worse than a black eye: "Cody's father / is being relocated for his job / after winter break and Cody / thinks long distance will be too hard" (271).

Part 3, Chapter 2 Summary: "Friday, December 14-Friday, February 8"

Xiomara, Xavier, and Caridad go to the Nuyorican Poets Cafe, and when the host "calls out the names on her list" (276), Xiomara hears her own name; Caridad has signed Xiomara up to perform a poem. As Xiomara waits for her turn, she watches the other poets "use their bodies and faces" (277). The crowd of 100 people claps in support when Xiomara hears her name, and when she is "done / saying a poem I've practiced / in the mirror, they clap" (279). Xavier tells her that she "'killed that shit'" (279), and the host of the open mic invites her to a youth slam to be held in February, the same one Ms. Galiano mentioned in poetry club. At home, Xavier "keeps turning to me in our room, / his face glowing" (281) with pride and joy, and "[t]he whole weekend [Xiomara] relive[s] the open mic" (283). In poetry club, the following week, Xiomara tells everyone that she performed at an open mic, and they all "seem amazed" (286). On the last day of school before winter vacation, Ms. Galiano tells Xiomara that she's "really blossoming" (287), and Xiomara agrees, knowing that her "poetry has become something [she's] proud of" (287).

On Christmas Eve, Xiomara goes to Midnight Mass with Xavier and Mami; when she gets home, she goes straight to her room, not expecting presents after the conflicts of the previous weeks. She is surprised when Mami enters her bedroom with a gift of jewelry; Xiomara assumes it will be a rosary, but it is "a small gold plaque / with my name etched on it, / a thin gold chain / making the bracelet complete" (291). To Xiomara's surprise, Mami has had Xiomara's baby bracelet resized so she can wear it now.

Xiomara acknowledges in a poem that "[t]he week after Christmas is the longest week of [her] life" (293). While waiting for school to start again, Xavier texts frequently with Caridad. Xiomara writes, reads, and edits her own work so often, she "begin[s] memorizing [her poems] by accident" (293).

On January 8, which is her and Xavier's birthday, the twins swap gifts, and Xavier gives her another leather notebook. Distracted by her anticipation that this day will be a good day, Xiomara leaves her old notebook on the kitchen table. She doesn't notice the notebook is missing until she gets to poetry club; as Xiomara prepares to leave the meeting in time to get to the church where Mami will be waiting for her, still believing she is attending confirmation class, Xiomara hears a voicemail from Mami that "spears ice into [her] bones" (299). Xiomara rushes out of the club meeting, knowing she will have to face Mami's anger once she gets home.

When Xiomara arrives home, Mami's rage makes Xiomara "shrink in the eyes of her wrath" (301). Mami has read her poems, the ones that Xiomara has written "for the people to read…without feeling guilt" (301). Xiomara is sorry "[t]hat she found it, that I wrote it, that I ever thought / my thoughts were mine" (302) but that doesn't stop Mami from trying to destroy Xiomara's poems by lighting the notebook on fire with a match. As Xiomara tries to save her poems, Mami "slaps me back hard onto my ass" (305), breaking Xiomara's recently-resized bracelet. As Mami recites Bible passages, Xiomara recites her own verses, "heaving the words like weapons from my chest; / they're the only thing I can fight back with" (305). Xavier and Papi interfere and save the notebook, but Xiomara is so upset that she leaves the apartment abruptly, with "nowhere to go / and nothing left" (313). She texts Aman, finally responding to his many apology messages, to see if he is free to meet her, and she calls Caridad to ask her to help Xavier, but she doesn't explain what has happened.

Xiomara waits for Aman on 168th Street. They walk together, holding hands, until Xiomara notices Aman is cold, wearing only a thin top and no socks. She suggests they go to his apartment, and "he raises both his perfect eyebrows" (320). As they go up the stairs to Aman's apartment, Xiomara thinks that "[a]ll the time we were together and happy I avoided coming here" (321). Once inside, Aman puts on "slow and soothing" music, and Xiomara tells him about what happened and that her poems "are a pile of ashes" (322). He says nothing, then "pulls [her] to him" (322). While embracing, they apologize to each other; as they kiss, Xiomara feels "b e a u t i f u l b e a u t i f u l / beautiful" (324), but when they are at a point where they're "lying on the couch / and he's on top of me" (326), she tells him they need to stop. She feels overwhelmed with feelings, including guilt "because he looks so / frustrated" (327), but the panic subsides as she thinks through "the knots inside" her (327). Xiomara is tearful, expecting Aman to call her what "girls get called in this moment" (328), but he simply wipes away her tears. Together, they cook food and watch YouTube videos, then doze off together in Aman's living room.

In English class the next day, Ms. Galiano notices that Xiomara is "wearing the same outfit as yesterday" (331). Xiomara's teacher explains that she had called Xiomara's house the day before when Xiomara ran out of poetry club so abruptly. Papi had "sounded frantic" (331) because no one knew where Xiomara had gone. Hearing that her father was worried makes Xiomara emotional, and Xiomara finds herself telling Ms. Galiano everything. Ms. Galiano hugs her and "tells [her] over and over: / 'Just breathe. Just breathe. / It's going to be okay. Just breathe'" (332). As Xiomara calms down, Ms. Galiano encourages her to talk with her mother and "figure out / how to make a relationship with her work" (333).

Though Xiomara is nervous and shaky at the thought of going home, she knows that she has the support of Isabelle, Ms. Galiano, Aman, Xavier, and Caridad: "although none of them can face Mami for me / I know I'm not alone" (335). On the way home from school, she stops at the church because she "know[s] assistance comes / in mysterious ways" (337), and when she comes home with Father Sean, she says to Mami that they "need to talk. / And I think we need help to do it" (338). Mami, "this woman who has been both mother and monster" (339), weeps and Xiomara hugs her, realizing that "love can be a band: / tears if you pull it too hard, / but also flexible enough/to stretch around the most chaotic mass" (340). Mami and Xiomara begin to meet with Father Sean once a week to talk; sometimes, Papi and Xavier join them, but "there's a lot [Xavier] doesn't say" (343).

Xiomara prepares for the poetry slam with Ms. Galiano and the other members of the poetry club. She is nervous that her poems are too personal, but Ms. Galiano tells her that "words give people permission / to be their fullest self" (345) in order to encourage her. Xiomara learns about the official rules of the slam and holds herself to her own rules, including "[d]o not give a disclaimer or introduction to your poem" (347), as well as the rules of the poetry club, including "[d]on't suck" (348).

The week before the slam, Xiomara practices her poem in front of her family, and both she and Xavier are "nervous / about how [their] parents might react" (349). When she finishes her performance, Xavier looks happy, "Papi claps"

(350), and Mami gives her unexpected advice, saying, "Speak up, Xiomara" (350). The day of the slam, Xiomara goes to the park with Aman, and after they listen to Nicki Minaj, he reads her a poem, his present to her. Aman's poem is "short and not very good / but I still blink away tears" (352).

At the slam, Xiomara "perform[s] like [she] deserve[s] to be there" (353), and Papi is proud of her. Xiomara observes that "[t]here is power in the word" (353). At home after the slam, Aman, Caridad, and the members of the poetry club join Father Sean and Ms. Galiano at the Batista apartment for a celebration; together, they enjoy food and music. Papi asks Xiomara to dance, because it "'is a good way to tell someone you love them'" (355).

The last piece of writing in the novel is an essay for Ms. Galiano by Xiomara about her favorite quote, which is Psalm 119:130: "The unfolding of your words gives light; it gives understanding to the simple" (356). In this essay, Xiomara writes about the metaphorical quality of the Bible that resonates with her understanding of poetry. She doubts she will "ever be as religious as [her] mother, as devout as [her] brother and best friend" (356-57), but for her, words have a power that is comparable to the power of religion and faith. She compares a poem to "[a] lantern glowing in the dark" (357) and describes "learning to believe in the power of [her] own words" (357) as "the most freeing experience of [her] life" (357).

Part 3 Analysis

The third part of the novel is full of ironically-meaningful moments that Xiomara shares with someone important to her. Though Xiomara's relationship with God is strained at the moment, she unexpectedly goes to Father Sean for help communicating with her mother. When Mami is enraged by the poems that reveal Xiomara's true self, Xiomara seeks comfort from Aman, the boy who has seen Xiomara at her most vulnerable. As Xiomara practices her spoken word performance in front of her family, Mami unpredictably encourages Xiomara to speak louder, wanting to hear more from her daughter after years of trying to silence her in the name of Catholic morality. All of these moments deliver emotional weight as the reader imagines how Xiomara must be feeling.

Part 3 also reveals Xiomara's resilience, even while she's in the midst of a significant emotional crisis. Even in Xiomara's weakest moments, at her most emotional, and even in her required English essays, she stays true to herself, knowing that her poetry will sustain her when life feels impossible. Those who encourage her as a poet— Xavier, Aman, Ms. Galiano, and the members of the poetry club—give Xiomara validation and confidence; eventually, Xiomara's persistence is rewarded, and even her parents are able to celebrate her talents with her and her friends.

The book concludes with a statement about the power of language. Words can hurt, but words can also heal, and Xiomara's talents enable her to understand the complexity of life as well as the ups and downs of all kinds of relationships. Love rarely promises to be easy, but sometimes, Xiomara learns, the deeper the hurt, the larger the capacity for love when resolution and forgiveness take place.

Xiomara Batista

Xiomara Batista is the 15-year-old writer of the poems that comprise the novel. She lives in Harlem with her parents and her twin brother, Xavier. Through Xiomara's poems, the reader learns that Xiomara's deceptively-quiet manner at school disguises a strong-minded and passionate nature. She will fight anyone who threatens her brother, and she is just as quick to defend herself when under pressure. Xiomara is also curious, intelligent, and eager to experience all that life has to offer. Xiomara has a mature and womanly "big-body" (255) figure that draws a lot of unwanted attention from men and boys, and she struggles to reconcile this with her own deepening interest in boys and dating. Xiomara's curiosity around the opposite sex meets with her parents' disapproval, especially her mother's: as the daughter of a devoutly Catholic mother, Xiomara is not allowed to date, which elicits resentment in Xiomara's. Xiomara writes poetry to find peace, to find her voice, and to create something beautiful from all of the pain and struggle she experiences while attempting to become the young woman she desperately wants to be. In her own words, "writing is the only way I keep from hurting" (41).

Xavier Batista

Xavier, Xiomara's twin brother, is older than his twin sister by fifty minutes. He is physically smaller than Xiomara, and he has a peaceful nature, in contrast to his sister's fiery personality. Xavier is also much more of a devout Catholic than his sister, which makes his sexuality a challenge for him at this stage in his life. Though Xiomara complains that Xavier has no "twin intuition" (100), Xavier is supportive of his sister and demonstrates love, generosity, and kindness towards her, especially when she is struggling with their parents. Xiomara calls Xavier "the worst Dominican" (98) because he does not like to dance and would "rather read / than watch baseball" (98). Xavier is unusually intelligent, and he goes to a school for gifted and talented students, where he meets Cody, who becomes his boyfriend and eventually breaks his heart.

Mami

Mami is a devout Catholic from the Dominican Republic; as a child, she wanted to grow up to be a nun. Her parents insisted she marry Papi, Xiomara's father, so that "she could travel to the States" (22). Her pregnancy with the twins was unexpected, and it happened after she and Papi had resigned themselves to being childless; the miraculous birth of Xiomara and Xavier contributes to Mami's high expectations of her children thanks to the supposed religious significance of their existence. Mami commutes a long way to work hard as a cleaner, and she is a strict parent to Xiomara, but less so with Xavier. That she treats her children differently based on their gender contributes to the tension between her and Xiomara.

Papi

Papi is a charming ex-womanizer who loved to dance. He kept up his antics while married to Mami but reformed once his children were born. He now works for the Transit Authority and travels back to the Dominican Republic regularly. Xiomara feels that even though he lives at home and eats meals with his family, he "could be gone as anybody" (65). She resents his emotional absence and the fact that he and Mami only talk to one another when they are discussing the twins. At times, Papi shows himself to be supportive of his children, such as when he interferes with

Mami's attempt to burn Xiomara's poetry notebook and celebrates with Xiomara after the poetry slam. Papi sometimes attends the family counseling sessions with Father Sean; on these occasions, Xiomara appreciates that he does stay and listen.

Father Sean

Father Sean, the head priest at La Consagrada Iglesia Catholic Church, has known Xiomara and her family for her whole life. He is originally from the West Indies and teaches youth Bible study and confirmation classes at the church. Because Father Sean appears to understand the challenges of being a young person, Xiomara does listen to him at times, despite her waning confidence in the guidelines put forth by the church. When Xiomara and Mami conflict, Father Sean looks for ways to support both of them; when Mami destroys Xiomara's poetry, it is Father Sean that Xiomara goes to for help.

Aman

Aman is Xiomara's biology lab partner and her first boyfriend. He is two inches shorter than Xiomara and though both of his parents are from Trinidad, he lives with only his father and speaks to his mother, who stayed in Trinidad, once a year on his birthday. Aman likes music and admires Xiomara's writing and performance skills. He is a gentle and affectionate young man, and he truly cares about Xiomara. When he fails to show his support at a critical moment, he apologizes over and over to Xiomara, demonstrating humility and genuine concern. Aman's nickname for Xiomara is X, and this nickname becomes both her stage name and the title of the novel.

Caridad

Caridad is a good friend to both Xiomara and Xavier, and she is a thoughtful and graceful foil to Xiomara's hot-headed character. Xiomara feels that Xavier and Caridad "are the ones / who act more like twins" (49), especially as the three friends have known each other their whole lives. Caridad finds it easy to live according to the rules of the church, unlike Xiomara, and she tries to help Xiomara whenever she can, lying to Mami to cover Xiomara and deflecting negative attention from Xiomara when there's trouble brewing.

Isabelle

Isabelle is Xiomara's straight-talking friend from poetry club. She is from the Bronx, and "she sounds / like a straight-up rapper" (257) when she performs her poetry for Ms. Galiano and the rest of the club. Isabelle's "curly blond fro" (267) leads Xiomara to believe she is mixed race.

Ms. Galiano

Ms. Galiano is Xiomara's English teacher. She is young and small in stature but "carries herself big" (37). Ms. Galiano is perceptive and caring; she patiently draws Xiomara out of her shell, insisting on high standards of work and inviting Xiomara to the poetry club repeatedly, until Xiomara finally attends.

Elizabeth Acevedo

Elizabeth Acevedo is the author of *The Poet X*, and there are many autobiographical elements present in the novel. Acevedo is a born and bred New Yorker of Dominican descent, and her interests in reading and writing stem from enchanting early childhood experiences with language. Her father was full of jokes and her mother told her stories from a young age, and this early exposure to the emotional power of words led her to the worlds of hip-hop, slam poetry, and, eventually, writing novels.

Guilt, Shame, and Religion

The feelings of guilt and shame mark many of Xiomara's difficulties with her mother, starting from a very young age. At age 11, Xiomara learned to link her own body with intense feelings of shame because her mother clumsily managed the arrival of Xiomara's first period. In her inexperience, Xiomara bought herself tampons without knowing how to use them. This decision horrified her mother, who hit Xiomara across the face. Mami felt at the time that tampons were only for women who were sexually active, and her actions only confused the innocent Xiomara.

Because Xiomara's period arrived much earlier than Mami expected, Mami was perhaps not prepared for the change. Possibly, she was also frightened by the fact that her daughter was developing so quickly. No matter the explanation for Mami's insensitive and borderline abusive behavior, Xiomara internalized her mother's assertion that "[g]ood girls don't wear tampones" (40). This early exchange may have initiated the intense conflicts that would soon characterize Xiomara's relationship with her mother.

Mami's Catholicism is a religion full of warnings and conditions, and these admonitions exist alongside its promise of love, peace, and heaven. Because Mami is such a devout Catholic, she does not allow Xiomara any space to doubt any of the cautionary tales Xiomara learns at church and in confirmation class. Rather, Xiomara is taught to feel guilty about her doubts and her seeming transgressions. Though Xiomara is a sensitive young woman, she is also an independent-minded one, and reacts to the pressures to feel bad about herself with indignation.

Growing Up and Separating from Parents

As 15-year-old Xiomara matures, her relationship with her parents (and her mother especially) changes and grows more complicated. Xiomara, like most adolescents, seeks a place in the world for herself, and her mother struggles to let Xiomara go. Xiomara's strict upbringing inspires a rebelliousness in her as well as deep feelings of resentment towards her mother and the church that her mother holds dear, so this natural separation between child and parent takes place in painful and difficult circumstances. Xiomara's need for independence is normal, but she lives in a world her mother perceives as dangerous. According to Mami, drugs, teenage pregnancy, and an adulthood full of disappointment and pain are Xiomara's inevitable future unless her daughter lives by Mami's strict guidelines.

Adolescent Sexuality

As Xiomara develops physically, she attracts more and more attention; men and boys are drawn to her in a sexual way, while some women and girls, like Xiomara's mother and some of her classmates, are threatened by her curves. She describes her physical transformation in her poetry, wishing she did not have "baby fat that settled into D-cups and swinging hips" (5).

These physical changes are accompanied by hormonal changes, so Xiomara finds herself looking at boys in a different way. When she begins a romance with Aman, her biology lab partner, she is scared and unsure about her feelings; together, they slowly explore their sexuality.

While Xiomara navigates the intimidating world of first love, her twin brother, Xavier, is doing the same. His situation is also complicated because he is attracted to boys.

Xiomara and Xavier know that both their conservative parents and the church would disapprove of Xavier's sexuality, but that knowledge does not stop him from starting a relationship in secret with a boy named Cody.

Xiomara's Baby Bracelet

In an early poem in the novel, Xiomara writes about her baby bracelet while describing what it's like to be born to older parents. In the same stanza, she describes the bracelet, engraved on one side with her name and, on the other, the phrase *mi hija* ("my daughter" in Spanish). It is her "favorite gift" (20) as a child, but it becomes "a despised shackle" (20) as Xiomara grows up and matures into an independent-minded teenager whose hopes are very different from the dreams of her devoutly Catholic mother. Xiomara's comparison of the bracelet to a shackle suggests that she feels handcuffed to her mother; from this trapped position, Xiomara fights against the restraint until she hurts herself and her mother.

As a surprise, Mami presents Xiomara with the bracelet on Christmas Eve, when "most Latinos celebrate" (289) and exchange gifts. Because they are in the midst of a conflict, Xiomara does not expect any gifts from her parents. When Mami gives Xiomara this unexpected present, she experiences mixed feelings. The baby bracelet has been resized for an adult wrist and it reminds both Xiomara and Mami of simpler times, when Xiomara was young and malleable and Mami was able to maintain her ideals about her daughter. To Mami, the resized bracelet might represent a hope that simply enlarging the bracelet will mean that Xiomara can wear it and stay her little girl; to Xiomara, the resized bracelet represents the dual sides to her person that are struggling to reconcile at this challenging time between childhood and adulthood.

Books, Poetry, and Other Literary Symbols

Throughout the novel, Xiomara uses imagery and symbols related to writing in her poems. By using words that have literary meaning in her own compositions, Xiomara is practicing with language; as a budding poet, language is her medium of self-expression, and only frequent use and experimentation will enable her to improve her writing skills.

Xiomara has a keen eye and ear for double meanings and metaphors, so her use of words related to books and poetry are powerful. For example, when describing her memory of getting her period for the first time, she communicates the depth of the impact of this experience with phrases related to writing: her first period, which marks her entry into womanhood, is "the ending of a childhood sentence" (39). The word "period," in this context, means both the punctuation mark and Xiomara's menstruation cycle, and this play on words reveals Xiomara's thoughtfulness and wit. With the arrival of her period, adulthood starts abruptly, a "phrase in all CAPS" (39), which is another way of saying she has undergone a powerful change, one that warrants emphasis and is echoed visually that the word "CAPS."

Xiomara's quickly-developing body inspires her to describe herself "like a myth" (48), or, more specifically, as "a story distorted" (48). The tale of Medusa inspires her; she imagines herself as the daughter of the snake-haired monster whose face can cause a person to turn to stone. This comparison reveals how Xiomara feels about her changing figure. Xiomara's curves cause a similar reaction as Medusa's eyes because they cause men and boys to stop in their tracks and stare at her in a sexual manner.

Xiomara also compares herself to a notebook whose binding is wearing out, causing the pages to fall loosely, while Xavier is compared to a book that is "award-winning" (99). Unlike Xiomara, Xavier doesn't get into fights and attends a special high school for gifted students. Ostensibly, he behaves well and according to the Catholic expectations of their parents, while Xiomara challenges the norms set by the church, creating problems and getting into trouble.

As her feelings for Aman intensify, Xiomara tries to make sense of them by comparing him to different kinds of writing; she does not see him as a sonnet, an old-fashioned poem written according to a rigid style, nor a haiku, a very brief poem that takes up very little space on a page. Also, it makes her happy that Aman's nickname for her, X, short for Xiomara, is a letter. All of these emotional and creative connections to literary matters emphasizes Xiomara's love for poetry and her unique writing voice and skill with language.

Hip-Hop Music

Xiomara and Aman both feel a deep connection to hip-hop music, as evidenced by their Friday afternoons in the park listening to albums by Canadian rapper and songwriter Drake and American rapper and songwriter Kendrick Lamar. These albums are meaningful to them especially because the songs are the soundtrack to their developing romance. Isabelle and Xiomara both feel an affinity for Nicki Minaj, born in Trinidad, (like Aman), so much so that Xiomara writes an essay about her for English class.

Hip-hop music has its origins in New York City, where African Americans and Latino Americans created the art form. That Xiomara, who lives in Harlem, loves this genre of music reinforces her characterization as an urban poet within the context of the novel. With her Dominican roots and her ear for rhythm and language, Xiomara's talent for performing spoken word links her with rappers and hip-hop musicians who also use their writing talents to communicate their experiences in the world to a larger audience.

Hip-hop artists use language creatively, much like Xiomara uses language in her poetry. They incorporate vivid metaphors, intense descriptions of emotion, and memorable sounds into the wordplay that makes their art so communicative and compelling to their fans. At the citywide poetry slam, Xiomara feels a deep satisfaction for having successfully performed her poetry to an appreciative audience; after all, much like the hip-hop artists she loves (and others who express themselves through language and musical rhythms), Xiomara "love[s] the idea of people listening" (344).

1. "Their gazes and words / are heavy with all the things / they want you to be." (Part 1, Page 21)

   Xiomara, the protagonist, writes of the pressure she feels as the teenage daughter of older immigrant parents who are religiously conservative. She feels unable to find her own path in life and to be herself when she is with her parents because they want things for her that she does not necessarily want nor understand. As well, her parents believe her birth to be a miracle, which only puts more pressure on Xiomara to be something she is not.

2. "But I stopped crying. / I licked at my split lip. / I prayed for the bleeding to stop." (Part 1, Page 40)

   Xiomara remembers experiencing her first menstrual period and buying tampons for herself at the age of 11. When her mother discovered that Xiomara was using tampons, she hits Xiomara across the face and accuses her of having sex, instead of helping Xiomara to understand what's happening to her body. Out of shame, fear, and confusion, Xiomara cries and prays that both the bleeding of her cut lip and her menstrual cycle will stop, as it is causing her difficulty she cannot understand.

3. "It happens when I wear shorts. / It happens when I wear jeans. / It happens when I stare at the ground. / It happens when I stare ahead." (Part 1, Page 53)

   In this poem, Xiomara acknowledges and confronts the unwanted male attention she receives due to her changing body. At 15, she is only starting to understand what it means to be a sexual being, and the male attention she receives alarms her and makes her feel powerless to convey an impression of herself that feels real. Grown men as well as boys show a sexual interest in Xiomara. As a result, she resents her own body for sending messages of sexuality she does not intend, and she resents the men and boys for making comments that she finds disturbing and unwelcome.

4. "I don't want to take / the bread and wine, and Father Sean says / it should always and be only done with joy." (Part 1, Page 60)

   Though Xiomara has grown up in the Catholic church, as she matures, she feels less connected to the conservative and judgmental elements of the religion of her parents. When Xiomara asserts her growing independence at church and refuses to take communion, her mother is not pleased. They argue about Xiomara's decision, and Xiomara uses Father Sean's words to defend herself, which only intensifies her mother's anger. Later, Xiomara decides to pretend to take the communion wafer to assuage her mother. She hides it under the pew nervously every time she commits the deception, feeling anxious about both defying her mother and disrespecting the body of the Christ.

5. "I don't breathe for the entire three minutes / while I watch her hands and face, / feeling like she's talking directly to me." (Part 1, Page 76)

   After Xiomara shows an interest in the poetry club but expresses confusion at the spoken-word element thereof, Ms. Galiano shows the entire English class a video of a woman performing her poetry. Xiomara is rapt; something about the woman's performance resonates deeply with Xiomara, and she feels as if her English teacher has given her a gift. This moment marks Xiomara's first exposure to the potential power of poetry.

6. "He is an award-winning book, / where I am loose and blank pages." (Part 2, Page 99)

    Xiomara uses a literary metaphor to compare herself to her twin brother, Xavier. He attends a gifted school thanks to his advanced intellect, and her parents treat Xavier due to his gender. Xavier is worthy of positive attention, symbolized by his analogy to an "award-winning book," while Xiomara is to be managed and organized and used for someone else's purposes. Her ironic use of the word "loose" to describe herself echoes the pressure Xiomara feels to be chaste while her hormones are surging and she is falling in love with Aman.

7. "He is not elegant enough for a sonnet, / too well-thought-out for a free write, / taking too much space in my thoughts/to ever be a haiku." (Part 2, Page 107)

    Here, Xiomara uses more literary metaphors to discuss her feelings for Aman. She equates him to poetry, which conveys the depth of her feelings for him; poetry, to Xiomara, is essential, so this series of metaphors communicates the high value of her relationship with Aman. In English class, Xiomara would have learned about sonnets and haikus, both poetic forms with old traditions and formats; she would have also written free-writes, a practice exercise with no parameters at all. Xiomara's first experience with love leads her to understand Aman as something original and poetic that does not fit into a category of writing she knows.

8. "I think it all just seems like bullshit. / So I say so. Out loud. To Father Sean. / Next to me, Caridad goes completely still." (Part 2, Page 119)

Ms. Galiano's poetry club meets on Tuesday afternoons, but Xiomara cannot attend because she must go to Father Sean's confirmation class at church. She resents this obligation, especially as she experiences this obligation just as she is questioning her faith in God and the Bible. At this moment, the confirmation class is learning that the story of Eve is a lesson in the consequences of temptation, and Xiomara is offended by the story because her life is currently full of so-called temptations that she wants to experience. Xiomara's friend, Caridad, reacts to Xiomara's expression of rebellious antagonism towards the parable of Adam and Eve with shock and fear, knowing that Xiomara's parents would react badly if they knew about it.

9. "Her center helped young women explain to their parents why they should be allowed to date, and go away for college, and move out when they turned eighteen…also, how to discover what they want to do in life." (Part 2, Page 127)

In this excerpt from a writing assignment for Ms. Galiano, Xiomara writes about topics that are important to her. This assignment is titled "Last Paragraphs of My Biography," and in this piece of writing, Xiomara reveals the tension she experiences at home and the oppression she feels under the influence of her parents.

10. "And I'm so glad he's changed the subject. / That I answer before I think: / 'I'm just a writer…but maybe I'd be the Poet X.'" (Part 2, Page 133)

While walking to the train after school with Aman, Xiomara tries to avoid talking about church. She feels that he will assume she is one of two church-related stereotypes: either she is too religious-minded to "do anything," or she is a repressed "church freak" (132). When Aman asks her about her interests, and she explains that she likes poetry, he wants to know what her stage name would be. She uses his nickname for her, X, to answer his question.

11. "Twin doesn't ask who I'm texting. / Though I know he's wondering / because I'm wondering who he's been texting, too." (Part 2, Page 136)

Xiomara and Xavier are closer than most siblings their age, and part of their closeness has to do with their being twins. When the twins are supposed to be asleep in the bedroom they share at home, both of them are texting someone else, someone who makes them smile and giggle more often than usual. Xiomara's intuition tells her that Xavier is texting with someone he likes in a special way, just like she is. For now, both twins respect the other's privacy, but soon they will both learn the truth about these late-night interactions over text message.

12. "I lean back against him, / feel his body pressed against mine. / 'Drake isn't the one that I like.'" (Part 2, Page 143)

Xiomara uncharacteristically suggests to Aman that they cut class when the fire alarm sounds at school.

While discussing their plan to cut classes, she says out loud to Aman what she has been thinking for weeks, foreshadowing an important step forward in their relationship: their first kiss. Xiomara reacts to the kiss with a combination of emotions, and her guilt, excitement, fear, and pleasure all make for several internal conflicts as she reconciles her desires with her parents' expectations for her behavior.

13. "I don't know what they would do / if the person he brought home was not a girl." (Part 2, Page 155)

Xiomara expresses concern on behalf of her twin brother, Xavier, whom she suspects is gay. Both of their parents are conservative and their mother is devoutly Catholic, so Xavier has good reason to be cautious about his sexual orientation. Xiomara worries about how their parents would react if Xavier were to one day be honest about his love and bring home a boyfriend.

14. "He's turned me into a fiend: / waiting for his next word / hanging on to his last breath / always waiting for the next, next time." (Part 2, Page 191)

Xiomara compares her intense attachment to Aman to a drug addiction. In this metaphor, Xiomara is able to express how she feels about the pleasure of Aman's company while communicating the sense of danger and risk that comes with such pleasure. This manner of describing the sense of longing someone experiences when in the thralls of first love suits Xiomara's urban life; drug dealers linger on the street corners of her neighborhood, so she is familiar with the danger of drugs and the risky pleasures they promise.

15. "Un maldita cuero. I am a cuero, and they're right. / I hope they're right. I am. I am. I AM." (Part 2, Page 205)

After Xiomara finds out that Mami has seen her kissing Aman on the train, she refuses to be shamed by her parents' anger and disapproval. While her father calls her cuero, *"[t]he Dominican word for 'ho'" (205), and her mother demands that she pray to the Virgin Mary for forgiveness, Xiomara insists to herself and to Xavier that she has done nothing wrong. Though her parents try to make her experiences and feelings seem small and insignificant, Xiomara resists their efforts to shame her, which only makes things worse.*

16. "How the stinging pain shoots up your thighs. / How you've never gritted your teeth this tight. / How it hurts less if you force yourself still, still, still." (Part 2, Page 212)

In order to encourage Xiomara to concentrate on her praying to the Virgin Mary for forgiveness, Mami has put grains of uncooked rice on the floor, which Xiomara must kneel on top of. The pain caused by the hard grains is intended to ensure that Xiomara links physical punishment to the fleeting and immoral pleasures of her embrace with Aman. While Xiomara is kneeling, Mami tells her that all men's hands are dirty no matter how tender their gestures. After this experience, Xiomara reflects on her experience with three poems, each of which are titled "The Things You Think While You're Kneeling on Rice That Have Nothing to do with Repentance." This excerpt is from the last of those poems.

17. "I push my locker closed and grill Aman before walking away. / 'That goes for you, too. Thanks for nothing.'" (Part 2, Page 220)

After dealing with her parents' wrath, Xiomara is distracted and withdrawn, and she goes to school with her spirit broken. That morning, in front of her locker, a boy molests her and pretends that it is an accident. Xiomara notices that Aman is nearby and that he has seen what has happened, and she assumes he will come to her defense. When Aman does nothing, Xiomara confronts and threatens her harasser herself and then "grill[s]" (220) Aman for his silence. In her abused state, Xiomara is unable to feel anything except pain and disappointment, and this moment marks a period of stubborn refusal to speak when Aman tries to engage her.

18. "His name is Cody. / And the poem was actually for you. / I thought it would be cathartic / to write something beautiful for yourself." (Part 3, Page 240)

Xiomara calls Xavier's boyfriend "White Boy," an epithet that reveals her own judgmental side. This racist epithet hurts Xavier, who gently retaliates every time this happens by telling his twin sister his boyfriend's name. In this moment, Xiomara's defensiveness is automatic; Xavier has just asked her to write a love poem, and she misunderstands, thinking that he wants to give it to his boyfriend. In her heartbroken and angry condition, she doesn't see any other explanation and the seemingly tactless request makes her angry. Xavier's kind and loving response has enough of an effect on Xiomara to inspire her to write a poem about it.

19. "I'll redo the assignment, if I can. / And I'll see you at the club tomorrow." (Part 3, Page 253)

Ms. Galiano has noticed that Xiomara's performance for English class has declined and that a change has come over her. Out of genuine concern, Ms. Galiano asks Xiomara to speak with her about a grade. During this conversation, Ms. Galiano invites Xiomara to poetry club once more. Even though Xiomara has previously decided to avoid getting in any situations that will cause more problems at home, she decides to skip confirmation class and attend the poetry club meeting instead.

20. "Us Batista twins have no luck with love. / You would have thought we'd be smarter / guarding our hearts." (Part 3, Page 272)

When Xiomara arrives home and sees Xavier in tears, she learns that Cody, his boyfriend, has ended their relationship because Cody's family is moving away from New York City. She tries to comfort him, and while offering her support, she expresses her feelings about their disappointment in love. Xiomara may also be talking about their difficult relationship with their parents; though Mami and Papi both show love to their twins, their love is complicated by high expectations and rigidity, teaching Xiomara and Xavier that love is not always simple and safe.

21. "I lay it across my wrist / and cinch the clasps closed. Her daughter on one side, / myself on the other." (Part 3, Page 292)

For Christmas, Mami surprises Xiomara with a piece of jewelry, and after all of the conflict of the earlier weeks,

*Xiomara is not sure how to react to the gift. Mami has resized Xiomara's baby bracelet so that Xiomara is able to wear it now, as a teenager. Xiomara observes her name on one side of the personalized plate and the phrase "*mi hija*" (my daughter) on the other side. The two sides of the bracelet reflect Xiomara's dual identity: one part of her is desperate to be herself, and this part of her is in conflict with the part of her that wants to obey her mother and fulfill all of her mother's desires for her daughter.*

22. "With Aman's soft breathing in my ear, / I think of all the firsts I've given to this day, / and all the ones I chose to keep." (Part 3, Page 329)

    Two weeks after Christmas, on Xiomara and Xavier's birthday, Xiomara accidentally leaves her old leather notebook full of her poetry on the kitchen table. Mami finds the notebook, reads Xiomara's poems, and is so upset about what she has read that she sets fire to the notebook in front of Xiomara. The destruction of Xiomara's poetry pushes Xiomara over an emotional ledge and she leaves home, texting Aman for support and then spending the night at his apartment. Xiomara stops them both before they go too far, and she reflects in this poem on her decision to maintain her virginity.

23. "Silent, silent crying that shakes her whole body. / And I am stuck, and still. / Before I go to her." (Part 3, Page 339)

    Xiomara returns home the following day after school and sees Mami in the kitchen. She tells Mami that she thinks that they need to talk and then she reveals that she has brought Father Sean with her, to help them discuss their differences and miscommunications. Mami is overcome with emotion, which temporarily stuns Xiomara into stillness, but she goes to her mother and embraces her. Though they are not yet able to speak the right words to each other, their hug is enough to start the healing process.

24. "Sometimes Twin and Papi come to the sessions / with Father Sean. Twin wiggles uncomfortably / in his chair. I know there's a lot he doesn't say." (Part 3, Page 343)

Father Sean helps Xiomara and her family talk through their issues. Though Xiomara is speaking truthfully with her mother and father about herself and her relationships, she notices that Xavier is not yet able to do the same. Instead of talking honestly about himself with their parents, he chooses to sit in his discomfort for his own reasons. Though Xavier is reticent, Xiomara and her parents are able to make progress on their relationship under Father Sean's guidance, which suggests that Xiomara does value his insight, though she may doubt other elements of the Catholic faith.

25. "Use your hand gestures a little less / and next time, en voz alta. / Speak up, Xiomara." (Part 3, Page 350)

Ironically, when Xiomara rehearses her spoken-word piece for her family before the poetry slam, it is Mami who suggests that Xiomara speak louder when performing. Many of the poems in the novel focus on Xiomara's inability to be true to herself and her need to silence herself and make herself smaller. As well, her relationship with Mami has been a source of difficulty because they disagree about so many important issues. Mami's advice to Xiomara to speak up reveals that Mami is finally interested in hearing from the real

Xiomara, not the idealized Xiomara she has created in her own image.

ESSAY TOPICS

1. Xiomara was delivered via caesarean section fifty minutes after her twin brother, Xavier, was born. Discuss the symbolism of this scenario from Mami's point of view.

2. The only pieces of prose in the novel are assignments that Xiomara has written for Ms. Galiano's English class. Compare and contrast Xiomara's prose style to her poetry style; what do the differences in style reveal about Xiomara's personality?

3. Write a character sketch of Xiomara's mother from the perspective of Caridad, Xiomara's oldest friend. Focus on the elements of Mami's character that Xiomara might find difficult to see.

4. When Xiomara refers to Cody as "White Boy," she hurts Xavier's feelings and reveals her own prejudices towards people who are different from her. Examine this side of Xiomara; where else do you see evidence of her bias and what causes her to change her views?

5. Research the parable of Adam and Eve. Then, write a version of the Bible story that would resonate with Xiomara, who balks at the notion of temptation.

6. At no point in this novel do any characters mention the word "feminist." Do you feel Xiomara would embrace the term, or do you think she would find the label difficult? Support your response with evidence from the text.

7. The novel engages with a number of important current issues that urban teens must face. Which is the most significant to you, and why do you feel this way?

8. Ms. Galiano is a positive role model for Xiomara. What similarities do they share and why is their relationship important for Xiomara at this stage in her life?

9. Much of Xiomara's poetry describes her relationship with Mami, but the reader does not get to know Papi in the same way. What sort of future relationship do you imagine Papi and Xiomara will have after the poetry slam?

10. Xavier faces challenges of his own as a young gay man from a Catholic, Dominican family. What kinds of expectations around masculinity are present in Xiomara's poetry that might prove to be difficult for Xavier?

Made in the USA
Coppell, TX
22 September 2020